Becoming a

Mom

A 14-Day Journey of Faith Through Miscarriage and
Infertility to Motherhood

Colleen Turner McGregor

Published by

PUBLISHERS

ISBN: 978-1-953759-86-3 (paperback)

To my beautiful daughter, Eliana, you are my daily reminder that God still answers prayers. You are my bump of blessing, my answered prayer, my rainbow baby and so much more. I love you dearly and will always pray for you.

Love,
Mom

Acknowledgments

To the Holy Spirit who has guided me and given me inspiration for the words written on each page, I say thank You.

I thank the Lord for taking me on this journey so I now have a story to share.

To my wonderful husband, Allan Jr., thank you for your unwavering support during one of the most difficult seasons of our lives. Thank you for believing in me and believing me, even when it seemed crazy.

To my dear friend, Melisha, thank you for always being my sounding board. I am grateful for your time, even if it was just to listen to me cry my eyes out on the phone. Your encouraging words back then are not forgotten. It was also you who ignited the fire within me to write this book. You told me, "Write the book and dedicate it to Eli." That was the spark I needed to start.

To my other soul sisters, thank you for understanding my pain even though it made for an awkward relationship at times.

To Lavern, for your obedience to the voice of the Lord, I say thank you. It is because of your obedience and boldness to speak God's word into my life, why I am now a mom.

Table of Contents

Introduction

I was that little girl who dreamed of getting married, having kids, and living in a beautiful home. The dream never included having a pregnancy loss or being diagnosed with infertility. *Becoming A Mom* was born out of the storms of miscarriage and infertility. While our journey may or may not be the same, I know the emotions are. The grief, brokenness, unworthiness, and jealousy, to name a few, are all the same.

Before you get started, I must say that this devotional is about my story that includes me later on conceiving and giving birth to my daughter. My story, however, is not intended to cause you pain and, please, do not think I am speaking to you with arrogance. I was once you, and though I have healed, the scars of miscarriage and infertility remain. I am writing this devotional to share with you a piece of me and the raw emotions I felt during the stormiest season of my life. I also want to share the power of God's Word and how faith in the Word brought me through to the other side.

Firstly, let me say that this devotional is not intended to mislead you into thinking that as soon as you speak the word, you will conceive. It took me months to see the manifestation of the word in my life, and for some people, years. No matter the length of time, we see that God remains faithful to His Word. The message I hope you get from this devotional is that God loves us and He gives us all we need for the season we are in. Even in the seemingly bad seasons of our lives, God's love is constant.

So, let's get started! Each day I share a part of my journey. The day ends with a thought for you to journal and then a prayer that addresses that part of the journey. At the end of the fourteen days, there is an encouragement for moms-in-waiting where I encourage you to seek the Lord's wisdom and be open to your options for other ways to become a mom. The devotional ends with affirmations. I absolutely love affirmations, especially those backed by scripture. I encourage you to declare these affirmations daily. Remember, Job 22:28a states "You will also declare a thing, and it will be established for you." (NKJV). Declare them and see how God works in your life.

Born to be Mommies

**"Lo, children are an heritage of the Lord: and
the fruit of the womb is his reward."
Psalm 127:3 (KJV)**

As a little girl, I always wanted to be a mom. I recall always playing with my dolls, feeding them, and putting "diapers" on them. In my mind's eye, I would always see myself with kids and living in a beautiful home. This became one of my ultimate life goals. As I became an adult, that desire grew stronger. Hearing my colleagues at work speak about their children truly melted my heart. My neighbour's kids would always stop by to say hi, and I could often be seen hanging with them. They would tell me about their day at school. We would play games and just have a grand time together. I cherished those little moments with them and prayed that I would be able to have those moments with my children one day. After all, God's Word reminds us that children are a heritage from the Lord and the fruit of the womb is His reward; I wanted that womb fruit too.

Although I had the desire to start my family, my husband and I were not ready. We cherished our time together as a couple but knew that one day we would have our very own family. Two of my closest friends (*my soul sisters*) were already mommies, and another was expecting her first child. I was truly happy for them and was extremely proud to see how they transitioned into the role of motherhood.

In 2012, I visited my gynaecologist because of the painful period pains I had. My husband picked me up from work and we both went. The doctor asked us when we plan on starting a family and what was holding us back. We looked at each other and thought nothing was holding us back and decided that we would start trying for a baby right there. Back then, we didn't have the fancy apps that tracked your period and fertility window, so the doctor took out a piece of prescription paper and recorded my dates as I told him. Based on the dates I gave, he told us when I would be most fertile and that we should try during that window.

When my next cycle was due but my period did not come, we eagerly went to get a pregnancy test. When the plastic stick showed a bright red "+" we were overjoyed. Overjoyed and shocked that on our first attempt we became pregnant. How easy was that?!

We were beaming. I had gotten my reward from the Lord, the fruit of my womb. I became extra careful with my body. I took my prenatal vitamins, ate well, did no lifting, and avoided anything that would have brought on any undue stress, well, except for the rigorous CFA exams that I was preparing for, for June of that year.

I was progressing so well; I had a grin on my face most times because I knew that life was growing inside me.

Thoughts

Do you think you were truly born to be a mom?
What makes you think so?

_____

_____

_____

_____

_____

_____

_____

_____

_____

_____

_____

_____

_____

_____

_____

_____

Prayer

Heavenly Father, thank You for the gift of pregnancy. Thank You for fulfilling that little girl's dream that I have always had to become a mom. Amen.

Day 2

Shattered Plans

"I will never forget this awful time, as I grieve over my loss."
Lamentations 3:20 (NLT)

It was Friday, May 11, 2012—a day forever etched in my mind. I recall going to the ladies' room only to discover what every expectant mom dreads, spotting. I panicked and called my husband to come and get me immediately from work. I called my doctor who said I should come and see him immediately. The car ride to the doctor's office was very long, well, that was how it seemed. I started asking God why this was happening to me as I was doing all the right things. I ate well, rested, and took my prenatal vitamins.

I was angry. I told Him about all those women who were not doing the right things while they were pregnant; they smoked and consumed alcohol, yet they carried their pregnancies to full term and delivered healthy babies. How could He have done this to me? He knew how much I wanted a child.

16

With all my questions to the Lord, I never heard an answer because, frankly, I was not listening. Actually, I didn't want to hear. I was angry and hurting.

When we got to the doctor's office, he ordered an emergency ultrasound. The radiologist was as cold as the gel she placed on my abdomen. She exhibited no emotions, it was as if she was not human. Her voice was unsympathetic as I asked her questions with tears running down my face. As she ran the transducer over my abdomen, I knew something was wrong. But although I had that gut-wrenching feeling that something was wrong, I still had an ounce of hope that maybe, just maybe, things were okay. I asked her "Is everything okay?" She indifferently responded, "Take back the report to your doctor. He will explain." I cried even more.

We took the report to the doctor and it stated that although I was twelve weeks along, the foetus was the size of a three-week-old. It became real, I was losing my baby. I broke down terribly. I felt like someone had taken away a piece of me. I felt deflated as I gasped for air. How could this be? All the plans we had for our baby were suddenly futile. I had lost a piece of me.

In his attempt to assuage the hurt we were feeling, he gave us the statistics that around 80% of miscarriages happen in the first trimester and it wasn't unique to me. He went on to say that these women who miscarry often go back and have successful pregnancies. This was of no help to me because my question remained: Why me? He then advised that we would be doing a dilation and curettage (D & C) the next day.

That night I hardly slept, not only because of the raw emotions but also because of the pain I felt as the clots came out. We got to the office early Saturday morning, the day before Mother's Day, to have the D & C done. How unfair was this? How could this be happening to me? The day before Mother's Day I was going in to do a D & C because I had lost my child. This was so unfair. I was placed under mild anesthesia, so although I felt no pain, I felt a tugging as he took out the remaining tissues from my uterus. When I opened my eyes, I saw my husband standing there looking defeated. He felt helpless as he could not do anything to help me or our baby. He cried, and that made me cry even more. We grieved our loss silently. It was truly an awful time for us.

The nights that followed were awful. Although I got painkillers, they didn't help. I had physical pain as well as emotional pain. My mom, mother-in-law, and maybe a few other persons knew about the miscarriage. We didn't share our loss with many people because it was so painful to re-live the moment each time we related the story. We felt alone; we felt as though God had left us with this burden to bear. I have not forgotten that awful time as I grieved my loss.

It was, however, in those times that we felt alone that God was really carrying us because I went to work the following Monday and carried on as if all was well with me. While life was continuing as normal, I was tearing up inside. No one knew the pain I was feeling, and I don't know how I managed to show up at work—it must have been God who took me through. I still carried on with my studies for the rigorous CFA exams which were a couple of weeks after the D & C. Although I did not pass that time around, I was proud of myself for still showing up and doing my best.

Thoughts

Have you ever lost a child? What were your
emotions? Did you feel as if God had left you
alone?

_____

_____

_____

_____

_____

_____

_____

_____

_____

_____

_____

_____

_____

_____

_____

_____

_____

Prayer

Heavenly Father, my spirit mourns, and my heart is shattered at the loss of my baby. You promised that weeping only lasts for a night, and joy will come in the morning. I pray for that morning time to come very soon because the nights seem so very long.

 Amen.

Day 3

Hurt

"Blessed are they that mourn: for they shall be comforted."
Matthew 5:4 (KJV)

My husband and I mourned the loss of our baby. He was, however, able to heal quicker from our loss than I did. I was stricken with grief. Now I truly understood what it meant to mourn the loss of a loved one. My baby, although only three months old, had become a part of me, and when I miscarried, a part of me left. I kept on asking God, "Why?" I was hurting badly. I became so easily triggered, I would break down for any and everything. If I saw any advertisement with babies, I would cry; if I saw a pregnant woman, I would cry.

My relationship with my closest friends began to suffer. As my friend progressed in her pregnancy, I distanced myself. After the loss of my child, I did not want to see her or could I speak to her anymore. My other friends were now in a position where they felt like they were walking on eggshells. They wanted to celebrate her pregnancy but had to be mindful of hurting my feelings. I decided that it was best that I shut off and just stay away. It broke my heart that I could not celebrate this huge milestone with my dear friend, but I was agonizing with pain that had nothing to do with her. I just could not face the reality of what my life would have looked like. Now all my closest friends either had a child or was with a child except me; this was hard for me.

My breakdowns became more frequent, and they lasted longer. At this point, I realized I needed help. My former manager, who is also a mom to me (momager), saw my hurt too and arranged for me to see a counselor. I would go to my counseling sessions on Thursdays after leaving work. I remember sitting and pouring my heart out to the counselor who I believed understood my pain. She spoke words of comfort and prayed for my husband and me. I told her about my friend who was expecting but that I could no longer speak with her because of my suffering. She advised me to write an email to my friend and express to her all that I was feeling and let her know that my distance had nothing to do with her. I did that and, thank God, my friend understood. She allowed me to grieve and gave me the space I needed.

My healing was very slow. I believed this was the case because I really wanted a child. When you truly yearn for something, and you get it, and then it is taken away from you, you experience a different level of hurt. I felt that my child was snatched away from me and that left me devastated. My pain turned into fear.

Thoughts

Have you ever been through a season of weeping?
Was there anyone who seemed to understand your
pain? Who was that person? How did they show
they understood what you were going through?

_____

_____

_____

_____

_____

_____

_____

_____

_____

_____

_____

_____

_____

_____

_____

_____

_____

Prayer

Oh God, thank You for Your comfort in this season of weeping. Thank You for placing people in my life who truly understand my pain and encourage me in moments of loss.

Amen.

Day 4

Fear

**"I sought the LORD, and he heard me, and
delivered me from all my fears."
Psalm 34:4 (KJV)**

As time progressed, my pain snowballed into fear, which was a dark place to live. Months later, the doctor gave us the go ahead to start trying again. However, I decided not to. I told my husband that I was too terrified of trying because I didn't want another miscarriage. I cried out to God and told Him my fears. I didn't think I could survive another pregnancy loss.

I knew this fear was not from God because it was so terrifying. I tried to remind myself of the scripture that says God has not given us a spirit of fear but of power and of love and of a sound mind (see 2 Timothy 1:7). On some days I felt good, on others I didn't; the fear would set in once again. But as I continued to hold on to 2 Timothy 1:7, the fear started to gradually subside. The Lord heard me and delivered me from my fears, and so we began trying again in November 2012.

So, unlike our very first attempt, we didn't get pregnant this time around. We tried again in December and again nothing happened. We kept on trying until November 2013 without any success. Although disappointed, we made nothing much of it. We just believed that the next time around we would become pregnant.

One day in November 2013, I began having period pains while at work. One of my colleagues told me about her gynaecologist who does heat therapy for period pain and she suggested that I see him because she thought it would help me. I agreed to see him and made an appointment. We saw him in December 2013 and told him about the terrible cramps that I was having. Of course, as a new patient, he wanted to know my medical history. So, we told him about our miscarriage as well as the fact that we have been trying for one year without being successful.

He ordered some tests for my husband and me. My husband had to do a semen analysis while I had to do a hydrotubation as well as an endometrial biopsy. We eagerly did these tests because we wanted to know why we weren't getting pregnant. Although we wanted to know why we weren't getting pregnant, we didn't think anything was wrong. After all, we were young and healthy.

Well, we were wrong!

Thoughts

Do you battle with fear? What is one thing you fear
the most?

_____

_____

_____

_____

_____

_____

_____

_____

_____

_____

_____

_____

_____

_____

_____

_____

Prayer

God, I am fearful. Fearful because I do not know what the future holds; fearful because I do not know if certain parts of history will repeat themselves. But thank You that when I seek You, You will deliver me from all my fears.
Amen.

Day 5

Distressed

**"Therefore my loins are filled with pain; Pangs
have taken hold of me, like the pangs of a woman
in labor. I was distressed when I heard it;"
Isaiah 21:3 (NKJV)**

Our results came back in January 2014. We
were excited about the New Year having set
new goals that we hoped to achieve with one
of them being to start our family. On the day we went
in to see my gynaecologist, we were so excited to
hear the results. He looked over them and told us that
my husband's results were very good, there were no
issues with him. On the other hand, he said my results
were not positive; the test showed that I was infertile.

I was filled with pain and distress when I heard it. I
cried. How could this be happening to me? I began
to question the diagnosis because there was
absolutely no way I could be infertile. I was young
and healthy. As a matter of fact, my period was on
time every month like clockwork, so how could this
be? He explained to me a condition called

anovulation which is what I had. So, although my period came every month, I was not releasing any eggs.

He was not perturbed, however, because he said there were tablets I could take to treat infertility. He told us about Clomid and prescribed them for me.

We filled the prescription and went home. I did my research on the tablets and saw where they were effective. Women even went on to have multiples after taking them. I was convinced; these were the pills that would cause me to become pregnant. I had now put my entire faith in the tablets. Despite my faith in the tablets, I was still hurting. I cried out to God and asked Him why this was happening to me. First, I lost my child, and now I was being told I was infertile. I grieved all over again for the loss of my child and now this shocking diagnosis.

I immediately started taking the tablets and, if you are anything like me, you love quick fixes. So, I took the tablets and expected that by the end of January we would become pregnant. Well, you can guess how that went—we weren't. When my period came, I was so devastated.

Thoughts

Can you recall a moment you felt distressed? What
was the cause of your distress?

_____

_____

_____

_____

_____

_____

_____

_____

_____

_____

_____

_____

_____

_____

_____

_____

Prayer

Dear Lord, be gracious to me in my distress. My eyes are worn out from frustration and my life is consumed with grief. Hear my prayer, oh God, and give comfort to my failing spirit.

Amen.

The Power of Your Words

**"Death and life are in the power of the tongue:
and they that love it shall eat the fruit thereof."
Proverbs 18:21 (KJV)**

My prayers and cries to the Lord increased daily. I felt like Hannah did when she was in the temple weeping and asking God for a son. At the time, I was not attached to a church, so I did not have the support of a small group to pray for me on days when I felt too weak to pray. However, I would always listen to Joel Osteen on Sundays, and on weekdays I listened to Joyce Meyer.

From Joel, I learnt about the importance of my words and that if I spoke positive words, then I would have positive results. So, I began to speak positive things over my life, like "I will have a baby." One morning Joyce Meyer did a teaching on Deuteronomy 28. At that time, I did not know what that chapter was about; however, it spoke about the blessings that God had promised the children of Israel if they obeyed Him, and the curses that would come if they disobeyed.

That morning, in particular, Joyce focused on the blessings and the only thing I remembered from that teaching was: blessed shall be the fruit of your womb. I took that promise God gave the Israelites and claimed it as my own. Every day I spoke that verse over my body.

I kept on taking the tablets and I kept on speaking the word over my life, but nothing changed physically. My tears continued. There were days when I had nothing else to say to the Lord but just to weep before Him. There were days when I spoke the word with so much faith and then there were days when I spoke with no faith behind what I was saying.

Unbelief sometimes kick in because when you are praying and believing God for something, and your current situation contradicts the very thing you're praying for, you'll begin to wonder. You begin to wonder if God will do what you're asking of Him. Not that He can't do it, you're just wondering if He will do it for you. There were many days I had those thoughts running through my mind.

I recall the story in the Bible when the father asked Jesus to heal his son. When Jesus told him that all things are possible for those who believe, the father responded saying, "Lord, I believe, help my unbelief." (see Mark 9:23-24). Those were my words many times. "Lord, I believe. Help my unbelief."

Not only did I battle with unbelief, but I went through a long season of emotional instability—feelings of brokenness and feeling "less than" were dominant. During the month I would feel so hopeful, expectant, and high on life, but as soon as my period came, those feelings would plummet. I would plunge into brokenness and despair. I didn't know that my period could have caused such feelings of brokenness; it was woeful.

I hark back to one morning while I was getting dressed for work. I'm not sure what triggered me but I broke down in tears. I called one of my dear friends and was just crying on the phone. I told her I was feeling less than a woman. This feeling was due to a definition I had created for myself of who a woman is. For me, a part of what makes you a woman is the ability to conceive. When I was not able to, it led to those feelings of inferiority. My friend listened as I spoke through tears. She never tried to dispel my feelings but rather showed empathy and offered words of encouragement.

Thoughts

Do you believe your words have power? Share an instance where the very thing you spoke of came to pass.

_____

_____

_____

_____

_____

_____

_____

_____

_____

_____

_____

_____

_____

_____

_____

_____

Prayer

Dear God, I know that my words are powerful but there are times when my situation contradicts the very thing I am speaking and praying about. In these moments, I ask that You remove doubt and unbelief and fill me with faith.

Amen.

Day 7

Faith Shifted

**"According as his divine power hath given unto
us all things that pertain unto life and godliness,
through the knowledge of him that hath called us
to glory and virtue."
2 Peter 1:3 (KJV)**

During my season of weeping, the Lord
brought me to a Bible plan on the
YouVersion Bible app called "A Seed of
Hope During Infertility." I do not remember how I
came across this plan but thank God that He always
gives us all we need pertaining to life.

The plan was for fifty-six days, and it aimed to help
you maintain hope during infertility. It gives
scriptures on the spiritual aspect of infertility, so it
included the stories of Sarah, Hannah, and Elizabeth.
It also had affirmations that were scripturally based
for you to speak out loud.

Every morning I got up and did the plan as my
devotion. With each day my faith grew, and my hope

was restored. I completed the plan on June 14, 2014. After completing the plan, I decided I would stop taking the Clomid. In hindsight, I believe it was the Holy Spirit who would have impressed this upon me because now my faith had shifted. My faith was no longer in the Clomid but now in God. As a matter of fact, I didn't think the tablets were working. We were now six months in, and I was not pregnant. Rather, it increased my menstrual cramps which were already bad before.

The shifting of my faith was due to the Word of God which I now knew. I now knew that Hannah, Sarah, and Elizabeth battled infertility, but God went on to bless them with a child. I believed that if He did it for them, He could certainly do it for me. So, it is very important to find the word that deals with your specific situation in order for your faith to be shifted. I told my husband about my intention, and he supported my decision 100%. I don't know if the support was because he truly believed God would make us pregnant or he just did so to please me because he saw my hurt. Either way, I am forever grateful to him for his unwavering support. I also told one of my in-laws about my decision. Out of her genuine care for me, she encouraged me to continue taking the pills because some women need a little "help." She also told me about a relative of ours who was on these same pills and got pregnant. I lovingly told her, "No, I'm just going to trust God" because that was where my faith was at.

So, in June, I stopped taking the tablets. I kept on praying, crying, believing, doubting sometimes, and speaking the word; my breakdowns continued, although not as frequent as before. My emotions were like a rollercoaster; the highs were good, but the lows were really bad. Despite my wave of emotions, one thing remained, I always went back to the Word, "Blessed is the fruit of my womb."

We still didn't get pregnant. There were days when my mind was saying I would have to adopt a child because I won't get pregnant. I cried even more on those days. While there is nothing wrong with adoption, that wasn't what I wanted for me. I wanted to conceive and carry a child of my own. Was that too much to ask of God? I didn't think so because I would always find testimonies of couples who were given a diagnosis of infertility but then they went on to get pregnant. There were also times when I wondered if I had to wait until I was in my nineties like Sarah did to conceive. These thoughts oftentimes increased my anxiety levels and I begged God just to give me the answer to my prayers immediately.

This would continue until November when a colleague said she wanted to speak with me.

Thoughts

Have you ever had your faith shifted? Share an instance where you desired to achieve something, and you thought that the only way to get it done was by taking a particular route but then in the midst of trying to achieve, you had to change routes.

_____

_____

_____

_____

_____

_____

_____

_____

_____

_____

_____

_____

_____

_____

_____

Prayer

Dear heavenly Father, thank You that You have given me all that I need for life and godliness. Thank You that despite me placing my faith in things other than Your Word, You have remained faithful in providing all that I need.
Amen.

Day 8

Word of Knowledge

"For to one is given by the Spirit the word of wisdom; to another the word of knowledge by the same Spirit;"
1 Corinthians 12:8 (KJV)

I used to stay back at work to study in the evenings. I had one colleague who was persistent in her request for me to visit her church. One week in particular, her church was having a crusade and she wanted me to come but I always turned her down because I had to study in the evenings. She said I could come on Friday evening because I normally do not study on a Friday. I told her I would not be able to because I was leaving the country the Saturday morning so I would have to go home and pack.

A couple of days after that conversation, she came to me and said she needed to speak with me. We went to a vacant office and she said, "Colleen, I don't know your business. I don't know anything about you, but the Lord said I am to pray for your womb."

Now this lady knew absolutely nothing about me; the most we spoke about was the news and weather, but God had given her a word of knowledge. When she said that to me, I responded with a poker face and said "Really?" because I was not about to tell her about my battle with infertility. This was due to pride and shame. Infertility is a topic that is not openly discussed; it's almost taboo. So, there was absolutely no way I was going to tell her what I was dealing with and, furthermore, we were not close.

She went on to pray. While she was praying, I said in my heart, "God, I receive this prayer because it must be from You since she knows nothing about me." When she was done praying, she said, "And the Lord said when you get back from vacation, you're going to get a bump of blessing." My heart fluttered when she said that. On the inside, I was very excited but didn't show it on my face. As I went back to my desk, I said to myself, "God, this must be true about the bump of blessing because the first thing she said to me about my womb is true, so this must be true as well."

At the time, the bank I worked at was acquired by another financial institution, and positions were being made redundant. I wanted to leave so badly so I had been hoping my position would have been made redundant. Now when she mentioned "bump of blessing" I took it as confirmation that I would receive my redundancy package. I was convinced that my redundancy package was on its way and no one except God could have told me otherwise. I thought to myself, what a blessing. God is so good! He had answered my prayer. I called my husband and told him that a lady just prayed for my womb and she also mentioned that I would receive a bump of blessing when I got back from vacation so it meant that I would be receiving my redundancy package.

I was excited. I was going on vacation and when I got back, I would receive my money. I had already called Human Resources for them to do the calculation so I knew the amount of money I would be getting. I made plans for this money. I would clear my credit card balance and do some investments that included the down payment on a home. God is indeed good, I thought to myself.

Thoughts

Did anyone ever share something with you about your personal life that only God could have revealed to them? What was it that they shared? What thoughts went through your head as they shared?

_____

_____

_____

_____

_____

_____

_____

_____

_____

_____

_____

_____

_____

_____

_____

_____

Prayer

Lord, thank You for the word of knowledge that You have placed in the heart of Your people. I pray that they will only utilize it for the furtherance of Your kingdom. I pray that I will seek discernment to know that this is from You and not dispel these words that may be necessary for my breakthrough.
Amen.

Day 9

Bump of Blessing

"And blessed is she that believed: for there shall be a performance of those things which were told her from the Lord."
Luke 1:45 (KJV)

I went on vacation in New York and had an amazing time with my mom, sister, nephews, and in-laws. It was such a joy to be with my family, although I was excited to get back for my bump of blessing. I had planned that as soon as I got my bump of blessing, I would take another trip back to New York and relax a little before I started job hunting again.

I got back from vacation after about two weeks of fun. One Saturday afternoon, as I was sitting in my living room while my husband was relaxing in the bedroom, I heard something deep in my spirit. I heard "Colleen, when women are pregnant, what do they say they have? A baby bump; that's your bump of blessing." I immediately got up and went to the bedroom where my husband was, and I told him that

I was pregnant. I told him what I heard in my spirit and that I believed. God told me, so I believed.

Now, it was not my time of the month. Based on the date that my last period came, my next cycle was not yet due and my period is always on time like clockwork. I didn't have any unusual feelings either that would cause me to think I was pregnant, but God told me and I believed Him. I believed Him because I was desperate; I desperately wanted a child. I desperately wanted to hear that I was pregnant. When you are believing God for something, you must take Him at His Word. You must have that "now faith"—the faith that is the substance of things hoped for, the evidence of things not seen (see Hebrews 11:1). I had no evidentiary support to my claim of being pregnant, but I believed.

My husband was excited and shocked, but he, however, believed me. Again, I don't know if he believed me because he genuinely thought I was pregnant or he did because he saw my desperation for a child. Nonetheless, I thank God for him and the support he always gives.

This revelation dispelled my original thoughts of what the bump of blessing was. Thank God I didn't tell anyone besides my husband about it. How embarrassing would that be? Here I was thinking about money and not knowing that what God had in store for me was exceedingly above what I was thinking.

As excited as we were, we decided not to tell anyone just yet. Well, that was until we had no choice but to.

Thoughts

Share one thing the Lord revealed to you that you
had no idea about. Did you believe when He told
you?

_____

_____

_____

_____

_____

_____

_____

_____

_____

_____

_____

_____

_____

_____

_____

_____

Prayer

Father, I pray that I will develop a deep relationship with You so I can always hear Your still, soft voice. I pray, Lord, that when I do hear that voice, I won't try to rationalize what You are saying to see if it makes sense. I pray that I will believe and be blessed and see the performance of the things You told me.
Amen.

Day 10

Crazy Faith

**"Seeing then that we have such hope, we use
great plainness of speech:"
2 Corinthians 3:12 (KJV)**

A couple of weeks after the Lord revealed to me what my bump of blessing was, I got an unpleasant medical diagnosis. I found out that I had a detached retina in my right eye that required urgent surgery. The surgeon wanted the procedure to be done under general anesthesia, so she made contact with an anesthesiologist and also sent me to my general practitioner for her to thoroughly examine me and give the go ahead for me to go under general anesthesia.

We got to my doctor and told her the reason for the visit. She did blood pressure checks, checked my sugar levels, and did a couple of other things. She also called another doctor to find out if I needed to do an ECG just to ensure my heart was healthy enough. The doctor told her no based on my age and previous medical history of being healthy. When she got off the phone, I told her I would not be able to do this procedure under general anesthesia. She asked why. I told her because I was pregnant. She asked if I missed my period. I told her no. She asked if I did a pregnancy test. I told her no. She then asked when was my last period; based on the date of my last period, the next cycle was not yet due. She began to look at me like I was crazy, but I could not blame her. I claimed that I was pregnant but had nothing to support that claim, except that God told me and I believed Him. I had so much hope in God and the word He gave me that Saturday afternoon that I spoke with great boldness to the doctor.

When I look back on that day, I realize that I had crazy faith—the kind of faith that doesn't make sense to the natural man. This was the kind of faith Noah had while building an ark despite there being no rain. I thank God for the spirit of boldness He gave me that day to open my mouth and tell this doctor who studies the human anatomy and is more learned than I am, that I was pregnant without any evidence. When the Lord told me what my bump of blessing meant, I never questioned it. I didn't try to rationalize it. I didn't do the logical thing which was to do a pregnancy test to confirm the claim. Before telling the doctor that I was pregnant, I never asked myself what if I was wrong. I didn't ask what if it wasn't

God who spoke to me but just my mind because I desperately wanted a child. I never asked any of those questions because I was sure it was the Lord who spoke to me, and I believed Him.

The doctor immediately ordered a pregnancy test. When the results came back, the stick showed a bright red plus sign that meant pregnant. She was shocked. I wasn't because I knew what I had heard in my spirit. She ended her examination there and told me what I had said to her, that the procedure could not be done under general anesthesia. I still ask myself, "What if I didn't open my mouth and tell her what the Lord had told me?" The doctor wouldn't have done a pregnancy test because my dates would not have suggested pregnancy. I would have done the surgery under general anesthesia and would have later miscarried. Lord knows I perhaps would not have survived that well. She, however, sent us to do an ultrasound, which I thought was not the wisest thing to do. Nonetheless, we went ahead to get the ultrasound done, and guess who was the radiologist? The same cold and unsympathetic doctor. She rubbed the gel on my abdomen and then ran the transducer over it. She kept on looking and looking but was not seeing anything. She asked me the date of my last period; based on that date, the next was not yet due. She then asked in an abrupt tone, "So why are you here?" I told her we just did a pregnancy test that was positive. She then went on to say, "Well, I'm not seeing anything." I got dressed and left immediately.

I contacted the anesthesiologist and told her I was pregnant. She asked me what my decision would be. In my mind, I thought, Isn't it obvious? There was no way I would harm my child so I would have to do the procedure wide awake. I contacted the surgeon and told her the procedure would have to be done using a local anesthetic because of my pregnancy.

Thoughts

Have you ever had a situation where you exercised
crazy faith? What was it? Do you want to be
remembered as someone who played it safe or
someone who trusted God and had crazy faith?

_____

_____

_____

_____

_____

_____

_____

_____

_____

_____

_____

_____

_____

_____

_____

Prayer

Dear God, I pray for a spirit of boldness—the boldness I need to pray crazy prayers so I can receive crazy results. Give me that crazy faith, the faith that will help me to always believe for the impossible and to choose hope over fear. Remind me, Lord, that it only seems crazy until it's done, so give me the courage I need to step out in that crazy faith in You.
Amen.

Day 11

Protected

"For he shall give his angels charge over thee, to keep thee in all thy ways."
Psalm 91:11 (KJV)

After informing the surgeon of my pregnancy, we went in to discuss how the procedure would be done and the risks associated with that. With local anesthetic, it meant that a lot of eye drops would be used to numb the area. The risk associated with that, she said, was that some of the drops could get in my bloodstream and ultimately to the foetus which can have an adverse effect. However, she said she would try her best to mitigate that happening. It also meant I would be wide awake but had to lay still, not even flinch for about two-plus hours. I thought to myself, how was I going to do that? Is it even possible to not move for two-plus hours while being wide awake? But remembering that there was life growing inside me, a baby I had prayed for, made it seem possible to do this impossible thing.

The days leading up to the procedure were filled with anxiety. I decided I would have to saturate myself with God's Word. I found all the scriptures on healing; I prayed them over my life and the life of my child. My favourite scripture was found in Psalm 91, the Psalm of protection. I would pray this daily and ask the Lord to give His angels charge over my child and me to keep us in all our ways, and that meant during the surgery as well.

Sunday, January 18, 2015, the day of my scheduled surgery. I remember only telling a few people about it. I was believing God for a miracle, and I didn't want to hear the what ifs. My friends and family are dear to me, and I know they mean me well. However, sometimes we get caught up with the natural that we try to reason everything out logically. During this period, I was believing God for the supernatural so I didn't want to hear about the side effects or about what could go wrong.

We got to my room, which was nice; it was almost like one of those 2-star hotels, which meant it was great for a hospital room. The nurse came and checked my blood pressure and my oxygen levels. My heart was pounding the whole time. I was anxious and scared; it was my first time doing surgery. I didn't know what to expect. I could feel my pulse at the side of my head. I was not doing well mentally but I knew I had to follow through. Not getting the surgery could have led to me losing my sight; I didn't want that for me or my child.

The porters came to get me. I had on my hospital gown, hair covering, and a pair of disposable shoes on. They also gave me a blanket because I may get a bit chilly in the theatre. It had become real. I was going in for surgery. My husband walked alongside as they pushed me on the bed. He went with me all the way until the nurse said, "You can't go beyond this point." He kissed me and told me that everything would be okay. I started crying. He was not beside me anymore. I suddenly felt lonely but then I remembered that God's angels were encamped around me.

The surgeon came and she tried to assure me that I would be okay. She had soothing music playing in the background, which I appreciated. She started with the numbing drops which were a lot. She had to ensure that I could not feel anything at all in the area. The procedure started, I could hear the clinging of the instruments and I could hear every word she and the nurses said. The entire time though I prayed back the scriptures that I had learnt about healing and especially Psalm 91. I kept my hand on my stomach as I prayed for my child's protection.

After two-plus hours, the surgery was complete without any complications. God's mercy kept us. He really did give His angels charge over us to keep us in all our ways.

Thoughts

Share an instance where you were in perceived
danger, but God protected you.

_____

_____

_____

_____

_____

_____

_____

_____

_____

_____

_____

_____

_____

_____

_____

_____

_____

Prayer

Dear Father, thank You for Your promises of protection. Thank You that You have given Your angels charge over me, to keep me in all my ways. May I always call upon You in my times of trouble.
Amen.

Day 12

A Sign

"And this is the sign from the Lord to prove that he will do as he promised."
Isaiah 38:7 (NLT)

I was on sick leave for about three weeks. Nobody at work knew why I was off, except for my manager who I told. I was very private about my life. My follow-up appointments showed that the surgery was a success. My retina was reattached, and my vision was getting better. God was good to us. During the period leading up to the surgery, I was in dialogue with my gynaecologist. I told him that my general practitioner had sent me to do the ultrasound even before my missed cycle, which he was surprised she did because it made no sense.

After the surgery, we visited my gynaecologist for him to do his checks and to ensure I was okay. He scheduled an ultrasound for us at six weeks. I had gotten very emotional over the weeks following the surgery. Although I had prayed and trusted God, there were still instances of unbelief. I kept on wondering if everything was okay with my baby and with my eye. Although my post-op visits were positive, there was still some anxiety in me. I especially wondered if any of the eye drops had escaped and entered my bloodstream and then to my child. I was filled with anxiety.

I returned to work and acted like all was well. At that time, I told a few persons the reason I was off; they couldn't tell I did surgery on my eye because, besides a little redness, there was no evidence that surgery was done. It was now six weeks and time for the ultrasound. Although I was excited, I was very apprehensive about what we would be told. I was still dealing with the trauma of the ultrasound I did that showed I was miscarrying.

Thank God this time around I didn't have to go back to that lady. My gynaecologist had a doctor who did ultrasounds right there in the office. We went in, she rubbed the gel on my abdomen and then started to move the transducer over my stomach while looking at the monitor. We heard the very strong heartbeat. I began crying; God was faithful. She kept on looking and moving the transducer. She then said, "What is that? Is that a limb?" My heart sank. I suddenly went back to that Friday afternoon when I was told I was losing my baby. I didn't know if seeing a limb was normal. I didn't know what that meant. The only thing I knew was that I went back to that place of hurt and devastation. All of this happened within five seconds. I asked the doctor if that was a good thing. She said yes. I then looked on the monitor and saw the limb of my child going up and down. At six weeks old, we saw my child's limbs moving up and down. I had no idea if this was normal or defied science but the doctor knew what she saw and she too seemed surprised.

When I got home, I thought about the whole experience I just had. It was at that time I realized that God was showing me a sign. He knew I was troubled in my spirit, that I was concerned about whether my baby was okay. So, the movement of her limb was to tell me, "Colleen, your baby is well." That was when I got the peace I yearned for and never worried after that if any eye drops had gotten into my bloodstream. God showed me a sign that proved He had done what He promised, which was to keep us in all our ways.

Thoughts

Were you ever bothered by a situation? Have you ever received a sign from the Lord about the thing that was bothering you? What was the situation? What was the sign?

_____

_____

_____

_____

_____

_____

_____

_____

_____

_____

_____

_____

_____

_____

_____

_____

Prayer

Father in Heaven, thank You that when I was troubled in my spirit, You showed me a sign—a sign that reminded me that You had heard my prayers and You are handling that which is troubling me. I pray that I will always pay attention to the little things You are showing me that are reminders of Your faithfulness, and not get distracted by the problems I face.
Amen.

Day 13

Ask, Believe and Receive

"Therefore I say unto you, what things so ever ye desire, when ye pray, believe that ye receive them, and ye shall have them."
Mark 11:24 (KJV)

Now that God had shown me that all was well with my baby, I went back to wondering about my eye. It was a constant battle in my mind that no one knew about. The negative thoughts would always come saying something was wrong or maybe the retina would detach once more. I was tired—tired of fighting this constant battle.

One day, a colleague of mine came and gave me a devotional book. As I opened it, it landed in the middle of the book. That devotional spoke about fighting battles. Just look at God! He knew what I was dealing with and provided what I needed. It went on to say that there are certain battles you can fight alone; however, there are others you need someone to stand in agreement with you because there is power in agreement. The reference scripture was

Matthew 18:19 which says, "Again I say unto you, That if two of you shall agree on earth as touching any thing that they shall ask, it shall be done for them of my Father which is in heaven." (KJV).

That evening when I got home from work, I sat and thought about the devotional. I knew the battle in my mind about my eye was something I could not fight alone; I needed a prayer partner, someone to fight with me. I started thinking about all the people who I knew were Christians who could pray with me. But as I listed their names, I began to cross them off. I wanted someone who had the faith to believe that God could heal my eye supernaturally. Each person I thought about, I thought to myself, "Nah, she won't believe with me" or "Nah, he doesn't have the faith."

So, I went to God in prayer. I told the Lord I wanted a prayer partner but not just any prayer partner, I wanted someone who had the faith to believe that He can heal me. I left my prayers there.

One Friday afternoon, as I sat in the kitchenette at work enjoying my lunch, one of my colleagues came in; he looked so excited. I asked him what was up with him. He said, "Colleen, I am reading this book." I interrupted and asked, "What book?" He said, "It's a T.L. Osborn book about healing, so if you see me acting crazy, it's because I have the faith to believe that God can heal anything." I almost choked on my lunch when he said that. I could not believe he used the same words I used in my prayer about who I wanted my prayer partner to be. God had answered! I said to him, "You are my prayer partner." He looked at me, paused, then said okay. I asked him for his number and told him I would call him to tell him why he was now my prayer partner. That evening I called him and told him about my eye because he did not know. I also told him about my pregnancy. From that day, we started having lunch together. We would read sections of the book from T.L. Osborn, the Bible and we would pray every day. We were believing God for this miracle together. I asked God for a specific prayer partner and believed that He would do it, and He did.

As time progressed, I got better at fighting the battles in my mind. I would use the Word, exercise my authority as T.L. did, and recall the testimonies. I realized that as I delved more into the Word of God, things got better for me. My pregnancy progressed without any complication and still only my manager and prayer partner knew about it.

Thoughts

Have you ever prayed and asked God for something
and He answered exactly how you prayed? What
was that specific thing? How did you react when
you received the answer?

_____

_____

_____

_____

_____

_____

_____

_____

_____

_____

_____

_____

_____

_____

_____

_____

Prayer

Heavenly Father, I thank You that if I ask and believe, I will receive. Thank You for the many prayers You have answered. May I always remain grateful and recall those past prayers that You have answered whenever I become doubtful about Your faithfulness.

Amen.

Day 14

He Answered

"Every good gift and every perfect gift is from above, and comes down from the Father of lights…"
James 1:17a (NKJV)

I wore my uniforms to work for five months. Yes, they still fit up to that point. I now felt that we were in the safe zone, so we could now tell other persons who were not extremely close to us. So, the first of those persons was my colleague who got the word of knowledge about my womb in November 2014. I pulled her aside one day and reminded her of the word she gave me back in 2014. I excitedly told her that I was now five months pregnant, and I thanked her for her obedience to the voice of the Lord. It was also at that point that I told her about the battle I had with infertility. I was no longer ashamed to talk about it because that shame had now become my testimony of God's goodness.

I also told another colleague who I observed had a close relationship with God. She was excited and prayed for me and my baby. She also copied a prayer from a prayer book she had called "Prayer for your unborn child." I prayed it daily over my child. I am truly grateful to God for her as she did encourage me throughout the remainder of my pregnancy.

At six months, I transitioned to maternity wear and the entire office now knew. Many were excited and offered encouraging words to me; if only they knew the journey. We did a second ultrasound to check on the fetal development and to also find out the sex of the baby. We didn't have a preference for the sex of the baby; all we wanted was a healthy child. For this ultrasound, I was not nervous, I was confident that He who began a good work will carry it on to completion (see Philippians 1:6). Everything was developing perfectly with our baby. Although uncooperative at first, we eventually found out the sex; our baby was a little girl. We were so excited!

My pregnancy continued to progress well. I enjoyed the kicks from her, which were my daily reminder that she is alive and doing well. One day while at work, I noticed I didn't feel the usual morning kicks. I went to the sickbay to lie down and to talk to her; still no kicks. BabyCentre had become one of my best friends, so I went on and searched for posts pertaining to "baby not kicking." I saw where some mothers suggested drinking a cold glass of water. That should get the baby moving. I did that, still no movement. I told my husband; we were both concerned. I started praying and reminding God of how far He had taken us, and I knew He wasn't going to leave us now. I decided to stay in the sickbay so no one would see the worry on my face. I fell asleep for about ten minutes. While asleep, I started to feel those kicks again. I started to cry and thanked the Lord. I was so happy! I called my husband and told him she was kicking again. A huge burden was taken off us both; we were relieved. We now realized that she was marching to the beat of her own drum and not ours. She moved when she felt like it and not when we wanted her to.

I decided to go off on maternity leave a week before my due date so I could rest and prepare myself physically and mentally for labour. At exactly forty weeks, my water broke some minutes after three in the morning. We rushed to the hospital thinking that she was about to be born soon. But my labour was long. It wasn't what I had asked the Lord for. I wanted a quick labour and delivery but that didn't happen. At about 4:30 pm, the doctor decided I had to have an emergency C-Section because I failed to progress, and my water had broken for so long, which meant the baby was exposed. Nonetheless, God remained faithful because although she was exposed for so long, she was never in distress.

She was born Monday, September 14, 2015, at 5:24 pm with a perfect APGAR score. She was our perfect gift from above. She was our rainbow after the storm—the storm of miscarriage and infertility. We named her Eliana, which means "God has answered" because that was exactly what He did. I prayed for this child and the Lord granted the desires of my heart.

Children are indeed a blessing from the Lord. At first, my husband and I were a couple, but now, with her, we became a family. She brought healing and joy to our home, and we give God thanks for His faithfulness.

Thoughts

Share the good and perfect gift that God has given
you.

_____

_____

_____

_____

_____

_____

_____

_____

_____

_____

_____

_____

_____

_____

_____

_____

_____

Prayer

Heavenly Father, thank You that You are a faithful God who lovingly hears and answers my prayers. I thank You for my gift, that good and perfect gift which is from You. Lord, on the days when I may feel doubtful or wavering about Your faithfulness, I pray that my child, who is my gift, will be a constant reminder that You still answer prayers.

Amen.

Encouragement for Moms-in-Waiting

I am truly grateful to God for the way my journey ended. God answered my prayers and blessed me with a beautiful daughter. However, I know that there are many moms-in-waiting, waiting for their little bundle of joy. There are moms-in-waiting who have prayed, fasted, declared the Word of God, tried Clomid and many other fertility drugs as well as IVF, but they are still waiting. I know exactly how you feel. I know the emotional instability you deal with, the feelings of unworthiness, the feelings of jealousy sometimes, and the feelings of anger. I have been there and battled all those emotions. I know that in waiting, it is sometimes hard to see God's faithfulness which then leads us to a state of hopelessness. I pray, however, that the Lord will restore your hope and give you peace in the waiting—that peace that surpasses all our understanding, the peace that confuses the enemy who will often bring thoughts of unworthiness and feelings of failure.

The enemy would want you to think you have failed yourself, your spouse, or even your family because you have not yet conceived. I encourage you, however, to dispel those lies and not lose hope in God's Word, which is truth. Isaiah 55:11 reminds us, "So shall my word be that goeth forth out of my mouth: it shall not return unto me void, but it shall accomplish that which I please, and it shall prosper in the thing whereto I sent it." (KJV). Let us continue to believe that His Word will not be void.

I pray that the Lord will send people in your life to provide comfort during this season as He did for me. I pray that the Lord will give you a sign for the things that are troubling you in your spirit, as He did for me. I pray that your faith is shifted like mine was; maybe you are thinking that your journey to becoming a mom is through pregnancy but the Lord has other plans. I encourage you to seek the Lord for His absolute wisdom; while you are believing God to bless your womb with a child, also be open to other avenues of becoming a mom, like adoption, fostering or surrogacy. God is all-knowing and He absolutely knows what is best for us, so although our journey may be similar, our stories may not always end the same.

Prayer

Father, I long to be a mother. I put my trust in You to help me conceive. I look to You daily for Your guidance and peace during this season of waiting. I pray for Your will to be done in my life. I also believe that, just like Hannah and Sarah, You can create in me fertile land. However, help me to be at peace if my journey doesn't end the same as theirs.

Amen.

Affirmations

The fruit of my womb is blessed (see Deuteronomy 28:4).

I keep my mind on Jesus and He gives me peace (see Isaiah 26:3).

I will trust in the Lord and not my own understanding (see Proverbs 3:5).

I will seek God for His wisdom about my circumstance, and I know He will give it to me liberally (see James 1:5).

What seems impossible with me and my doctors is possible with God (see Matthew 19:26).

Infertility is not too hard for God (see Jeremiah 32:27).

To have a child is a good thing, and God promises not to withhold any good thing from me (see Psalm 84:11).

God's promises to me are Yes and Amen (see 2 Corinthians 1:20).

God promises that if I worship Him, He will bless my bread and water, and I will not miscarry or be barren (see Exodus 23:25-26).

Whatever I ask for in prayer, if I believe I will receive (see Mark 11:24).

My words are powerful and so I choose to speak life to my womb (see Proverbs 18:21).

I am blessed as I continue to believe in God's Word (see Luke 1:45).

Like Sarah, I believe and declare God's promises over my life and by faith I receive His strength (see Hebrews 11:11).

I call the non-existent things as if they were, so Lord, I thank You for making me a mother (see Romans 4:17).

Colleen Turner McGregor is a Christian, wife, mom, and pregnancy loss and infertility survivor from Kingston, Jamaica. After her first miscarriage, she struggled with infertility. Her resolute faith in God was rewarded as she later went on to conceive and give birth to her rainbow baby, Eliana. Colleen has a heart for moms and those waiting to become moms, so she delights in supporting them through scripture and words of encouragement. Colleen holds a Bachelor of Science degree in Banking and Finance from the University of the West Indies, Mona, has passed Level 1 of the CFA exams and works as a Securities Analyst.

You may contact Colleen at:
colleenwrites876@gmail.com

Made in the USA
Monee, IL
20 July 2023

39621583R00056